AMERICA'S RAILROADS

TRAINS

Lynn M. Stone

The Rourke Corporation, Inc.
Vero Beach, Florida 32964

PHOTO CREDITS:
Cover, p. 4, 7, 8, 13 © Lynn M. Stone; title page, p. 15, 18 from East West Rail Scenes; p. 10 © Don Hennen; p. 17, 21 © George H. Drury; p. 12 courtesy of Union Pacific Railroad Museum Collection

PRODUCED BY:
East Coast Studios, Merritt Island, Florida

EDITORIAL SERVICES:
Penworthy Learning Systems

Library of Congress Cataloging-in-Publication Data

Stone, Lynn M.
   America's railroads / by Lynn M. Stone
      p. cm. — (Trains)
   Summary: Surveys the history and uses of American railroads, how they work, the different kinds, and the current state of the industry.
   ISBN 0-86593-519-X
   1. Railroads—United States—History Juvenile literature. [1. Railroads.] I. Title. II. Series: Stone, Lynn M. Trains.
HE2751.S69 1999
385'.0973—dc21
                                    99-13276
                                         CIP

Printed in the USA

TABLE OF CONTENTS

TRAINS

Trains are made up of **locomotives** (LO kuh MO tivz) pulling or pushing railroad cars on tracks, or rails.

Trains haul people and **freight** (FRAYT). Freight includes all kinds of products, from autos and oil to coal and corn.

Locomotives, or engines, are traveling power plants. Each locomotive is run by an engineer who rides in the **cab** (KAB).

The United States has more miles of railroad track than any other nation.

RAILROADS

A railroad, or railway, is a company that operates trains. The United States and Canada have three types of railroads. The largest of these are Class 1. The U.S. has eight Class 1 roads and Canada has two.

The 32 American regional railroads are much smaller than Class 1 railroads. Most of them, however, have at least 350 miles (560 kilometers) of track.

The smallest railroads are the 500 or so local lines.

6

The Union Pacific Railroad travels over some 36,000 miles (57,900 kilometers) of track, more than any other American railroad.

HOW TRAINS WORK

A train engineer does not steer a locomotive. A locomotive's wheels simply follow the track.

A railroad track is made of two steel rails. Each rail is laid exactly 4 feet, 8-1/2 inches (1.44 meters) from the other. The rails are held in place by wooden or concrete **crossties** (CRAWS tiez).

Each train wheel has a rim on its inner edge. The rims keep the wheels from slipping off the rail.

Railroad car wheels have a rim that
helps keep them on the rails.

THE FIRST RAILROADS

The first railroads in North America began in the early 1830s. These early trains were all in the East. They were pulled by small, steam-powered locomotives.

When the first trains appeared in North America, there were no airplanes or cars. People depended upon horses or their own two feet for transport on land.

Trains were loud and strange, but they were very useful. They could move large groups of people and thousands of pounds of freight. And they could do it faster and better than horses!

Steam locomotives brought a new and important form of transportation to North America. Steam trains helped America expand quickly to the west.

11

In May, 1869, the tracks of the Central Pacific and Union Pacific Railroads met in Promontory, Utah. The event marked the beginning of railroad service from one coast to the other.

Bridges known as trestles allow trains to pass over rivers and canyons.

By 1835, over 1,000 miles (1,600 kilometers) of railroad track had been laid in 11 states. By the mid-1850s, railroads went from Chicago to the big eastern cities. Along the rails, new cities sprang up. The nation grew with its railroads.

The U.S. Government began giving land to railroads, helping them to grow quickly. By 1869, a person could travel by rail across the continent, from California to New York.

Railroad activity helped build Chicago. The city, America's third largest, became a center of the rail industry.

LOCOMOTIVES

During the 1800s, bigger and better steam locomotives appeared. By the 1860s, steam trains could race along at 60 miles per hour (97 kilometers per hour), though not for great distances.

In the late 1800s, the first electric locomotives were used. Electrics were powered by electricity. They did not need to burn coal or oil.

Electric locomotives were most useful near big cities, where electricity was plentiful. Unlike steam locomotives, electrics did not dirty the air and countryside with smoke and flying sparks, called **cinders** (SIN derz).

The Pennsylvania Railroad's classic GG1 electric locomotives served from 1935 into the 1980s.

Steam locomotives ruled most railways until the late 1930s. By then, diesel-electric locomotives had appeared.

Diesels were powered by diesel oil. Diesels started and stopped faster than steam trains. They ran at higher average speeds. They cost less to run and less to keep running.

By 1960, diesel-electric locomotives had taken over main line railroads in the United States. Today, most locomotives are diesel-electric. The others in regular service are electrics.

Diesel-electric locomotives, like this Alco PA, had replaced most of America's steam power by 1955.

CHANGING TIMES

North Americans depended upon railroads for transportation through the 1920s. Railroads then began to lose some of their importance. Cars, trucks, and buses had arrived.

By the 1950s, American railroads were losing millions of dollars with their passenger trains. People were driving or flying instead.

In 1958 the U.S. Government allowed the railroads to stop passenger service that was losing money. The railroads did, and passenger service on private roads soon disappeared.

Amtrak took over passenger service from America's failing private railroads, like the Gulf, Mobile, and Ohio, shown here.

AMERICA'S RAILROADS TODAY

America's railroads have become fewer, but the industry is gaining strength with its freight service. Each day thousands of locomotives and cars shuffle freight from one city to another.

Several regional railroads run short-distance passenger trains called **commuters** (kuh MEU terz). And Amtrak, started by the U.S. Government in 1970, operates several long-distance passenger trains. The clickety-clack of wheels on steel still echoes over 170,000 miles (274,000 kilometers) of American rails.

GLOSSARY

cab (KAB) — the part of a locomotive where the engineer and others ride to operate the controls and view the tracks

cinder (SIN der) — bits of burned or burning coal that rises out of a steam locomotive's smoke stack

commuter (kuh MEU ter) — a passenger train that carries people between large cities and their suburbs

crosstie (CRAWS tie) — a flat piece of wood, metal, or concrete used to support and hold rails

freight (FRAYT) — goods and products transported by shippers, such as railroads

locomotive (LO kuh MO tiv) — a power plant or engine on wheels used to push or pull railroad cars; a train engine

INDEX

FURTHER READING

Find out more about trains with these helpful books and information sites:
Riley, C.J. *The Encyclopedia of Trains and Locomotives.* Metro Books, 1995

Association of American Railroads online at www.aar.org
California State Railroad Museum online at www.csrmf.org
Union Pacific Railroad online at http://www.uprr.com

BLU